What My Mama Told Me: Life, Love, and Legacy

A Collaboration Led By
Regina Sunshine Robinson

What My Mama Told Me: Life, Love, and Legacy
Published 2026 by Regina Sunshine Global Network LLC

Compiled by Regina Sunshine Robinson
Contributions by Co-Authors
Christine Adams
JoAnn Bellamy
Marchell R. Gause
Toureign A. Terry-Hunt
Angela Jean-Louis, Ph.D.
Dr. AudreyAnn C. Moses
Clintoria Session
Debbie Woodbury, MPA, SHRM-CP, CPRP
Cover and Layout by Jawad Ahmed Khan
Edited by Charlotte Ehney
Edited by Pamelia Stanley
Introduction by Charlotte Ehney

Paperback ISBN: 978-1-971991-02-3
Ebook ISBN: 978-1-971991-03-0

For information:
Regina Sunshine Global Network, LLC
www.ReginaSunshine.com

Dedication

To all the Mothers and Daughters that need this book…May this help you to remember what you have, to cherish what you were given, to love when it's hard, to forgive when it's necessary, to cherish every moment, to hug every chance you get, to laugh when you want to cry, to be who you both need, and to never let go. If you are still here, there's still time to say I love you.

And to every daughter who's here without her mother, she's with you in ways no one can truly explain. Although her physical body is gone, she lives on in what she told you with her words and the life she lived before you. It's not easy, but I'm sure she would tell you, "Baby, keep on living."

And to my mother, I'm still trying to make you proud. As always, it's never goodbye for us. I'll see you later.

Regina

Table of Contents

Introduction

From the moment of our conception, our mothers are our first human contact. We nestle protected within their wombs. At our birth, our mothers nurture and guide us. For some of us, whether by necessity or choice, another woman steps into the role of mother to take care of us. These mothers shape us with their love, discipline, and guidance.

Within the chapters that follow, daughters honor their mothers. They recount the lessons, care and strength that shaped who they eventually became. They share the depths of their love for their mothers and, for some, the ache of loss at the death of their mothers. They share the dreams passed to them that they in turn pass on to their own children.

It has been my privilege to read these accounts, to hone the words conveying the memories and lessons, and to set these tributes on the pages that follow so we can all learn from What My Mama Told Me.

Charlotte Ehney
Editor

Chapter 1

Love Personified

By

Regina Sunshine Robinson

Love Personified

Geraldine Alford Gore

"Servant of God"

> "Love is patient, love is kind. It does not envy, it does not boast, it is not proud. It does not dishonor others, it is not self-seeking, it is not easily angered, it keeps no record of wrongs. Love does not delight in evil but rejoices with the truth. It always protects, always trusts, always hopes, always perseveres. Love never fails."
>
> I Corinthians 13:4-8 NIV

I've always said that I learned to love people by watching how my mama loved people. I have also said that I have been loved so much in my life that it pours out of me and into others. And that is because of my mother. She was love on fire. So many people's lives would be changed forever if they had a head on collision with love because real love always makes the difference. And I know real love because of the mother I was blessed to have. I would choose her a million times over to be my mother, and I am forever grateful God chose her for me. I couldn't think of a better way to honor her in this book than to share the words I spoke at her homegoing service. Below are my remarks from that day.

“Love Personified”

Giving honor to God, Pastor Hill, Reverend Vereene, Pastor Alford, Rev. Murray, and all other ministers, family, and friends. I didn’t know if I would be able to do this today. But how could I miss the opportunity to speak and honor the woman who started me out speaking. She always loved to hear me speak. It was a dream of hers to hear me speak at Mitchell Sea. This past August her dream came true as I was a speaker at a women’s conference here, and she sat right over there. She was so proud and full of love. Thank you, First Lady Davena Hill, for making that dream come true.

My mother Geraldine Gore was Love Personified. She was love. She gave love. She showed love. She was everything I knew love to be in the earth. And although our hearts are broken, I want to remember the parts of her that felt like love on fire.

If nothing else in this life, she loved.
She really loved.

She loved:

- She loved People.
- She loved Serving.
- She loved Cooking.
- She loved Cookbooks…She read cookbooks like other people read novels.
- She loved Magazines.
- She loved Tennis…Like she watched the tennis channel all day.
- She loved Football.
- She loved the Pittsburgh Steelers.
- She loved Carolina…Let's be clear, UNC Chapel Hill. Not that fake Carolina down the road in Columbia.
- She loved Drawing.
- She loved Marching Bands.
- She loved Singing.
- She loved Luther Vandross.
- She loved Lionel Richie…I say more than Luther, but my sisters don't agree.
- She loved Pepsi.
- She loved Ginger Ale…Canada Dry to be specific.
- She loved Talking.
- She loved Spades…I believe she, Ms. Nellie, Ms. Mamie, and probably Harold Riggins are having the spades game of a lifetime today. I hope Mama and Ms. Nellie are winning. Sorry Rod!
- She loved Reading.
- She loved Fishing.
- She loved Earl….We all know she loved Earl.
- She loved her Truck.
- She loved her Home.
- She loved Laughing.
- She loved Crushed Ice.

- She loved Sweaters.
- She loved Dooney & Bourke.
- She loved Seeing My Hair Straight…My mama sure didn't like my natural hair. I got it blown out today for her.
- She loved Plum Lipstick.
- She loved Burgundy Nail Polish.
- She loved Meeting New People.
- She loved Speaking Her Mind.
- She loved Meatloaf.
- She loved Salad Bars…Because she was gonna put every single thing on that salad bar on her salad.
- She loved the Color Purple…Not the movie.
- She loved Pens…I got this from her. I will scoop up a great pen at an office sign in.
- She loved Dogs…especially Chihuahuas.

Can anyone think of anything she loved?

But most of all she loved:

- She loved Head Start.
- She loved Kingston Lake.
- She loved Mitchell Sea.
- She loved Her Pastor. Pastor Hill, she was so proud to have you as her Pastor.
- She loved her friends… And there are too many of you to mention by name. I thank you for loving my mama.
- She loved Her Family.
- She loved James Alford, Sr.
- She loved "Snook" Elizabeth Alford… she loved herself some Snook.
- She loved Cassie Bell and Geneva.
- She loved James, Wille, Donald, and Ronald… Them Alford Boys.
- She loved John.
- She loved Jessica.

- She loved Jr.
- She loved Gabriel... the first grandbaby, she said she never knew she could love anybody like that.
- She loved Christian.
- She loved Nicholas.
- She loved Olivia… her only granddaughter.
- She loved King… Little James Alford as Earlisha says.
- She loved Vicky.
- She loved Zoe.
- She loved Pamelia.
- She loved Earlisha.
- She loved Me.

But above all she loved God! And His Love gave her the power to love the way she did.

Geraldine Gore was a reminder that love is an action word and real love always makes the difference. She was the love of my life. Our family will never be the same again. The original Sunshine is gone. She was tired and decided to rest. She got a glimpse of heaven and chose to go be in the presence of the King.

Mama, I'll see you later. It's never goodbye for us. I always say it's not over til I win. If I haven't won yet, that just means it's not over. Well Mama, it's over. You won. You ran your race. You finished strong. You earned your rest. And we rejoice in your Well Done.

Until we meet again…I hope you dance with Jesus. I hope Grandma made you some sweet potato bread. And I hope you and Ms. Nellie get a Boston today.

Affirmation: I AM LOVED.

Regina Sunshine Robinson

CEO, Regina Sunshine Global Network LLC

Regina Sunshine Robinson is an Empowerment Specialist and the CEO of Regina Sunshine Global Network.

She is the author of two books, a 3-time *Chicken Soup for the Soul* Contributing Author, Acclaimed Motivational Speaker, Award-Winning Talk Show Host, National Workshop Presenter, Professional Business Coach, Certified Educator, and Accomplished Publisher. Regina hosts the *Finding My Way Back with Regina Sunshine Podcast* and *The Regina Sunshine Show* on the RSGN Channel on Status Network.

Regina has been the recipient of many awards. In 2018 and 2019, Regina was presented with resolutions from the Georgia House of Representatives, and in 2019 and 2020, she was recognized from the House floor for work in youth empowerment and media. In 2019, she received the Distinguished Georgia Citizen Award from the Secretary of State's Office and was inducted into Who's Who in Black Atlanta. Regina's motto is "It's not over til I win," and she wins when she sees others WINNING!

You can connect with Regina at www.ReginaSunshine.com.

Chapter 2

My Forever Angel

By
Christine Adams

My Forever Angel

Annie Elizabeth Adams

"The Best Homemaker/Big Momma"

> “God grant me the serenity to accept the things I cannot change; courage to change the things I can and wisdom to know the difference.”
>
> Serenity Prayer

Annie Elizabeth Loyd became Annie Elizabeth Adams when she married my dad, Eugene Adams, on June 13, 1960. My momma wasn’t just my mommy; she was my angel here on Earth. She has been there for me countless times, but with all my pregnancies, she was my rock.

My first child Christopher (her baby) was born on December 20, 1991 and was her favorite grandchild (LOL!). The back story on this one is that when my mom was pregnant with me, she thought I was a boy, so she had only one name, Christopher. I turned out to be a girl, so she named me Christine. When I became pregnant with my first born, she asked me to name him Christopher. I did, and he became her favorite grandchild although she denied it (LOL!) just like she denied spoiling me.

On February 12, 1996, I delivered my second son, Shaun, by C-section. My mommy and daddy drove from Alabama to New York because my mommy knew I needed her. Due to complications from the C-section, the incision didn’t close and became infected. I had to have a nurse come out morning and night. In between those times, my mommy learned how to clean my wound (a fish’s mouth, as she called it).

That would not be the first or last time she would be by my bedside in a hospital. On October 16, 2008 while pregnant with my 4th child, I was given the devastating news that my baby was a stillborn. My mommy sat by my bedside from October 17th until October 19th when I would finally give birth to Nathaniel.

My mommy was the best mommy anyone could have, and I am thankful God gave her 84 years to be with us. You can never prepare for the devastation of losing a loved one, especially a parent. Losing my mommy crashed my whole world. Nothing is ever perfect. My momma and I had some challenging moments with me growing up and wanting to do what I wanted to do regardless of what my momma said. As a teenager, I fought and fussed with my momma until I turned 18 years of age. At 18 years old, I understood what others were saying "you only get one mother" meant. I wrote my momma a letter apologizing to her for what I put her through and always making her cry. From that point on, I cherished my momma. Now I'm not saying I stayed obedient because I would be lying if I said I did (LOL!). I was spoiled and my momma knew she spoiled me and would get offended when any of my siblings would call her out on it (LOL!). I spoiled her too, always being there for her when she needed me. I've always told her and my dad that I could never repay them for what they did for me and my sons, but I would do anything within my power.

In 2019, my momma was diagnosed with breast cancer. At this time in my life, I had married again and was living between states but would later understand God allowed this diagnosis in order to remove me from a situation. I took care of her until she was back on her feet and able to do for herself. My momma taught me about love, family, and resilience but she was never the same after that cancer diagnosis. The vibrant woman that I had known my whole life was now a vulnerable, frightened, and depressed woman. Her body was going through so many changes as she grew older, and she was having a hard time dealing with it. In 2020, the Pandemic caused her to become more afraid. My momma became less affectionate so I could no longer get my hugs and kisses on the cheek. May 22, 2023 would be the last time I got an "I love you" from my momma. I dedicate this poem to her:

In the clouds I see your face
In my mind I hear your voice
In my heart I feel your presence
In the clouds where there is heaven
You are resting peacefully
No more pain, tears, and sadness
No more worries, no more sleepless nights
In the clouds
The little girl in me wants my mommy
And the adult in me wants my best friend
Missing our talks
Your laughter too

And the way you smiled
On the days you could
In the clouds
You will be
Away from me physically
But your spirit will live on
In every memory and moment shared,
In every lesson learned and love given
So here's to you, my beloved Queen
Sending love and gratitude to heaven,
For the time we shared
In the clouds.

Crissy

Affirmation:

I AM GRATEFUL FOR MY NURTURING SPIRIT AND THE POSITIVE IMPACT I MAKE IN MY FAMILY'S LIVES.

Christine Adams

Author and Podcast Host

Christine Adams is a passionate author and podcast host dedicated to inspiring confidence and authentic connections.

She has authored three impactful books:
Sexual Appetite: The Love of A BBW,
Sexual Appetite: The Second Helping,
and a devotional journal created to uplift and encourage. Currently, she is working on a heartfelt new book titled *Letters To My Mommy*, dedicated to her beloved mother.

As the host of a newly created podcast *Talking Thick With Chrissy*, she creates a safe space for thick conversations on life, love, body positivity, and personal growth. Guided by her motto "Thick conversations with real connections," Christine aims to empower others to embrace their true selves and foster meaningful relationships through honest conversations and shared experiences.

Chapter 3

My Mother

By
JoAnn Bellamy

My Mother

Rosa Lee Bellamy Terry

"Home Maker, Retiree"

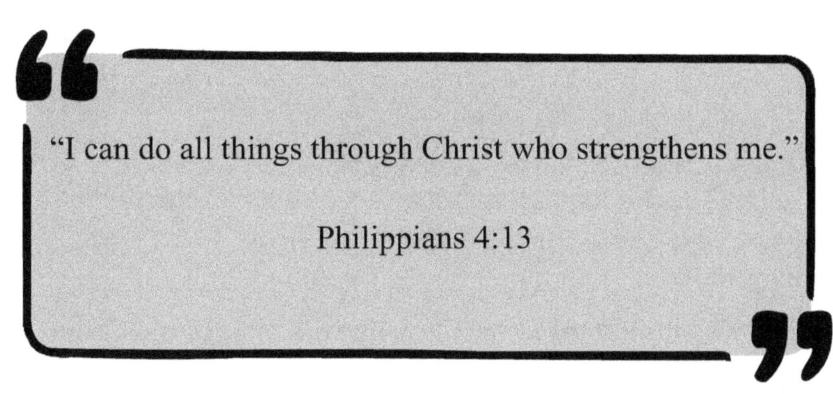

My mother is a 4'5" petite woman with a caramel complexion, small built body, and naturally curly hair. She is a lovable, fiery, and strong-willed woman. My mother is the oldest girl of seven children. She took advantage of life, raising a baby girl with her six others serving as at home babysitters. Even though she only has an eighth-grade education, she is very determined. When I reached the age of three, Mama married my stepfather. He was 5'7", medium complexion, lumberjack built, family oriented, and a very hard worker.

I Corinthians 13:11

Love:

During my childhood, I watched Mama work hard in the hot fields from sunrise to sunset. She also scrubbed other people's floors and houses. She worked in these situations to make sure I had essentials and school necessities. Monday through Saturday she endured back breaking sweat, but she would always attend church on Sunday and never complained. Mama taught me how important it is to attend church.

My Mother

Philippians 4:19

Education was important to Mama; she was always old-fashioned and believed in punishment. Rain, sleet, hail, or snow, school was number one. Every day before school she would say, “Get up and get ready for school.” Then after school she would say, “Take your school clothes off, eat a snack and do your homework.” She was strict, saying, “I have a switch that will tear your tail up, if you don’t.” I was afraid because that sharp and loud tone sounded like thunder and lightning.

Mama was an inspiration to others as well as me because of the way she treated others and expected the same demeanor from them. She meant what she said and said what she meant. At school, I was known as the little girl with a mama that would speak her mind. Being an only child, she was extremely protective of me. Mama’s love taught me to be respectful and to respect others, to educate myself as long as I can, and to love others, as well as myself.

2 Timothy 2:15

When I would get upset with Mama, I would repeatedly say, “I don’t care.” This would upset her. Mama would reply, “Stop and NEVER say that again!” I knew Mama meant BUSINESS. Her constant reminders taught me to care about people. This was a change in my life. She taught me to care and love unconditionally no matter what.

Mama is the smallest, strongest woman I know. Two years ago, Mama had heart surgery due to leaking in both of her heart valves. Mama never complained. Three months later she was diagnosed with breast cancer and again never complained. God brought her through three months later; she completed a three-month cardiopulmonary rehabilitation program on an exercise bike to strengthen and improve her body. The next year, her faith was tested yet again. A trip to the ER turned into a hospitalization due to her blood glucose fluctuating from 32 to 517, vomiting, and hemorrhaging. She even developed Clostridioides Difficile. Mama never complained. After a week and four days, she returned home. She was full of energy and able to dance at the senior citizen prom.

Matthew 9:20-21

Legacy:

I have never seen Mama worry about NOTHING!!! And told me to NEVER WORRY!!! (Unlike me, she has no gray hair on her crown). Even while writing this, Mama's health was declining from not walking to inclining on a rollator to walking faster than before.

I honor her STRENGTH: Good days or bad days, she never complained.

I honor her FAITH: In sickness or good health, she kept believing.

I honor her COURAGE: She weathered the storms and kept standing strong and being a warrior.

I admire her SELF-RESILIENCE: Tough and elasticity, Mama inspired me to keep my head up regardless of anything in my past.

God blessed me with biological and bonus moms. My bonus mom Mrs. Theresa Goss Singletary's favorite quote was "Mark My Word," meaning what she said, good or bad, would happen.

I honor her WISDOM: She left past and future guidance.

I'm so grateful for her ADVICE: She imparted everlasting words of knowledge.

She shared her unconditional love and always had a listening ear for me.

These mamas inspired the same to thousands of women around the world. They encouraged others to seek God first and move forward. I'm proud to be the daughter of these mamas with these qualities and to pass them on to my daughter, Shapora.

The memories of sacrifices, hardships, experiences, knowledge, courage, happiness, survival, faith and love are values that lead into the next generation. "A MAMA knows her past, understands her present and moves toward the future." Philippians 4:13

Affirmation:

I AM SOMEBODY AND AM LOVED.

JoAnn Bellamy

Author Motivational Speaker

JoAnn Bellamy was born, raised and currently resides in Columbus County, North Carolina.

She is a homemaker, motivational speaker, single parent of one daughter and caregiver for her mother. She holds a degree in Business Administration and is currently a full-time college student pursuing a degree in Audio/Video Production Technology. Her tribulations and hardships have given her a strong desire for knowledge. She was a 2025 nominee for the prestigious Dr. Dallas Herring Achievement Award.

Her life reflects Dr. Herring's philosophy of "Taking you where you are to carry you as far as you can go." She enjoys public speaking, church, traveling, movies, beaches, dining out, quiet relaxation moments, and spending time with family. She also has a special love for animals.

You can connect with JoAnn through her website at www.Joannsjourney.com or email at JoannBellamy23@gmail.com. You can find her on Facebook, Instagram @iamjoann23, and Tik Tok @JoannBellamy717.

Chapter 4

The Gift of Sight

By
Marchell R. Gause

The Gift of Sight

Marcella Gause

The Gift of Sight

According to loved ones, my biological mom, Marcella, read to me while I was still in her womb. Sadly, I'll never get to hear her personal sentiments—she passed away when I was four, just five days after my birthday. My memories of her are vague, and I sometimes wonder if they're truly my own or tender recollections gifted by others.

For as long as I can remember, I had a book in hand every chance I got. Even now, reading is a daily ritual—something that brings me peace and perspective. Between the lines of countless pages, I've found joy, understanding, empathy, and connection. Reading has allowed me to glimpse the lives and hearts of people far different from me and yet somehow humanly familiar.

Throughout every chapter, I developed a deep respect for words. Over time, I realized my love for them was planted long before I could speak. My mother spoke something sacred into me—a gift I now carry with gratitude. Though she hasn't been here to nurture it for 39 years (and counting), what she instilled has taken root and grown. If her storybook words could shape me, how much more powerful are the eternal words of God?

"Before I formed you in the womb I knew you, before you were born I set you apart…" (Jeremiah 1:5). My mother taught me the power of words and vision, even in her earthly absence. But God, in His grace, didn't leave me motherless.

The Gift of Sight

Nellie Gause Vereene

Into the space grief left behind stepped my maternal great-aunt, Nellie —who became "Mommy" in every way. Her love was old-school. She believed children should listen more than speak and stay in a child's place. Still, her approach wasn't unkind—it was structured, steady, and deeply intentional. She was fiercely protective and loved hard from a big heart. Though her love wasn't always spoken softly, her presence was sacrificial and sure. She loved her family, her church, and her community. She cooked, served, sowed seeds, praised, and prayed. And even as her health declined, she did so with grace and unshakable faith.

Less than a week after Thanksgiving 2017, my mom suffered a stroke that stole what little vision she had left from diabetic glaucoma. From that moment until her final breath in 2021, she lived in total blindness. And while we adjusted to caregiving—and quietly grieved the shift in our family dynamic—she continued to live with intention: hearing every voice, feeling every presence, and praying with a faith that filled the room. Even in the hardest moments, she never stopped believing.

I often find myself repeating one of her favorite sayings: "Just keep living, baby." But more than her words, I remember her example. She taught me to show up, no matter what. To love as an action. To walk by faith. To extend grace, even when it's hard. And to embrace a motherly heart—a lesson I've had to live out in spirit, not biology.

"For we walk by faith, not by sight" (2 Corinthians 5:7). That verse lives in me differently now, after watching my mom embody it day after day.

Maya Angelou once said, "People will forget what you said… but they will never forget how you made them feel." I didn't always have the words to explain it as a child, but I never forgot how Nellie made me feel—safe, secure, covered, and cared for. And though I don't remember many of Marcella's words, I've never forgotten the imprint of her love either.

One inspired me to visualize; the other showed me how to endure.

My Mothers taught me to see—not just with my eyes, but with my spirit. One gave me a love for words; the other taught me to live them out. One planted the seed; the other nurtured its growth. They both showed me that even in loss, I am never alone.

I carry and honor both of their legacies. Although life revised my story early on, I was surrounded by the vision, love, and faith of women who taught me not just how to survive—but how to overcome by seeing with my spirit and walking in the truth of my testimony.

Their lives told me things words alone couldn't fully express.

Affirmation:

I AM ROOTED IN LOVE AND STRENGTHENED BY FAITH.

Marchell R. Gause

Marchell Gause is a certified life coach and commercial underwriter. With over 15 years in the insurance industry, she brings the same thoughtful discernment to her professional work as she does to her personal calling—encouraging others to live with intention and compassion.

A proud aunt and mentor, Marchell finds purpose in volunteering as a sighted support for Be My Eyes, an organization that helps people who are blind or who have low vision, and serving through SisterTalk, a peer-led initiative for mental health advocacy and women's empowerment.

Whether helping others reframe their narratives or walk through hard seasons, she creates space for people to feel seen, valued, and supported. She lives in North Carolina and finds joy in music, reading, and being present for those she loves. Her work reflects her core belief: healing begins when we own our stories, walk in truth, and make space for others to rise with us.

Chapter 5

Nappy Hair Is Happy Hair

By
Toureign A. Terry-Hunt

Nappy Hair Is Happy Hair

Harawese R. "Peaches" Somayah
Moore Kambui-Khaliq

> “Love from the fullness of your heart through the depth of your soul.”

The song began "Nappy hair, nappy hair…" My mother was a revolutionary songwriter for adults and children. I always knew she had a beautiful singing voice, and she surrounded me with songs that celebrated my unique, black beauty as a child. It was the 70s, a time when black culture was rising up with personal pride and challenging the conventional image of beauty.

Today, as I comb my natural hair and feel the burn in my arms, the song whispers back to me:

Nappy hair, nappy hair
It just don't get no air
But when the sun
comes out to shine
I am so thankful
you are a daughter of mine

Nappy Hair Is Happy Hair

My mother, Peaches or Sister Somayah to her beloved friends, taught me that nappy hair is happy hair, and happy hair is healthy hair. She taught me self-love and self-care through song rather than preaching, although she did that too. I remember her songs more than her words. She was not always songs and sunshine; sometimes, her words hurt me even though she said them in love. My mother was fierce with her words and could use them to cut and scar or liberate and heal.

She would verbally disapprove of me wanting straight hair and denounce anyone telling me in her presence that I was lucky to have "good hair." She would look at my straightened hair and express her disappointment, saying things like, "It looks dead." All the while, she'd remind me that I did not need my hair "fried and laid to the side" after hours of getting it pressed out. But this was her way of loving me; loud approvals and disapprovals.

Nappy hair, nappy hair
It just don't get no air
But when the sun
comes out to shine
I am so thankful
you are a friend of mine

When I was around other children, my mother changed the song slightly. She would hear them comparing each other's hair and wishing they had something different. This saddened her; she witnessed their minds being washed with hate and hopelessness. This was before we transitioned into pre-teens; a time when our young minds were still being molded into what is good, bad, and ugly in the world and how we fit into the larger society.

Looking back, I realize how wise my mother had been to sow seeds of self-love and acceptance by teaching us that we are magnificently created just the way we were born. I am who I need to be today because she shared and showed her power and beauty. As a member of the Black Panther Party in the Los Angeles chapter, I witnessed her fighting and enduring police brutality. She marched and stood side by side with political leaders, Hollywood stars, and neighbors to celebrate black pride through equal rights and fair equality. She was an inspiration to many people of color because of the many trails she set ablaze. How could she not, being an Aries, the fire sign?

Now, I'm taking my mother's lesson of self-love to heart, especially when it comes to my daughter, Skye, and her hair journey. I often find myself echoing my mommy's wisdom and even her words when I speak to Skye. I encourage Skye to speak kindly to herself, to embrace her hair texture even when it seems unmanageable, and to take breaks when her arms get tired from combing her afro puff. It warms my heart to see myself in her. I wonder if my mother saw herself in me too, and that's why she was so fierce in encouraging a strong self-image in me.

The words of wisdom that I now pass on to my daughter wrap her in the same blanket of love for who she is and who she is becoming. I feel blessed to be able to recall moments that bring back that love and wisdom from my mother. My love journey continues to evolve with life, but one thing I know for sure is that my hair will always be loved through its life and death moments – from my bouncing brown youth to my rebellious stages of wild purple shades, and even when my crown sparkles with gray. I'll always remember my mother's words:

> Nappy hair, nappy hair,
> It just don't get no air
> But when the sun
> comes out to shine,
> I am so thankful you
> Are a daughter of mine

I'll continue to carry on her words of wisdom so Skye can inherit them, know them, and cherish them. Because that's what mothers do – they teach their daughters to love themselves, and to pass that love and wisdom on to the next generation; to their daughters, their daughters' daughters, and their daughters' daughters' daughters. Our love will carry on forever.

Affirmation:

I AM A BLACK ROSE, BEAUTIFUL AND BOLD.

Toureign A. Terry-Hunt

Transformational Coach, Author and Facilitator

Coach Hunt, also known as Toureign Angelina Terry-Hunt, MS, is a passionate transformational life coach who is dedicated to empowering women in building a stronger connection with self-love. She believes in uncovering her client's true potential and guiding them towards a purposeful, joyful, and connected life through her framework of L.O.V. E.

Coach Hunt's coaching sessions are personalized for each individual, as she focuses on identifying and addressing the unique obstacles and issues that may be hindering her clients from feeling fulfilled. Her approach combines introspection, self-awareness, and practical tools, empowering her clients to recognize and embrace their strengths and overcome their limiting beliefs and insecurities.

With a deep commitment to her clients and an unwavering passion for growth, Coach Hunt creates a supportive space for them to explore and develop their ideal definition and design of self-love through aatheart ®.

Chapter 6

Keep Living: Life Sayings From My Mama

By

Angela Jean-Louis, Ph.D.

Keep Living: Life Sayings From My Mama

Annette Cain

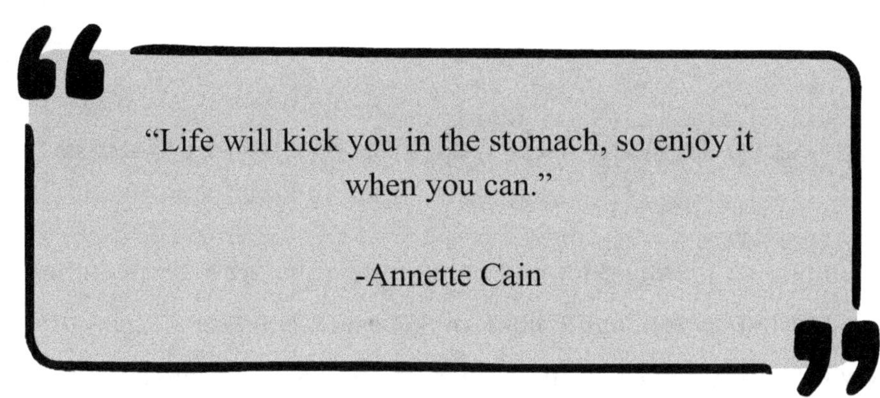

My mama, Annette Cain, was born in 1941, part of a generation of women who didn't have time for nonsense—complaining was just "wasting breath." Raised on a dirt road by my sharecropping grandparents, she was baptized in hardship and sharpened by life's trials. With deep faith and fierce responsibility to family, she taught me that survival was strength and wisdom was wealth. And the truth? Church hat on or off, that wasn't optional—whether you wanted to hear it or not.

At 84, my mother is very aware of her mortality. She's buried friends, outlived my father, and even lost my older sister just a few years apart. She often says, "I have one foot in the grave and the other on a banana peel." When I asked her what that meant, she reminded me, "The Bible says seventy years are promised" (Psalm 90:10), so she knows she's living on borrowed time.

But that hasn't slowed her down one bit. She's busy living—attending Sunday School, serving on the Mother's Board, going out with girlfriends, traveling with family, shopping, enjoying movies, or just sitting quietly in her favorite chair. She often tells me how grateful she is to drive, cook, and live independently in her house.

Of course, in classic Mama fashion, she says with blunt honesty, "I hope y'all take me outta here in a casket because I am not living anywhere else!" Her lesson is clear: even when you're standing on the fragile line between life and death, you don't have to crumble. You live, and you live well.

"Watch how a man tips. It will show you if he's generous or stingy." My mother never missed a chance to remind me that generosity isn't just about money—it reveals a person's heart. She always said one reason she fell for my daddy—besides his good looks—was his kind, giving spirit. In my eBook, *How to Use the Power of Visualization to Thrive on Purpose,* I share how my mama's wisdom shaped my vision of love. She told me to see the kind of man I wanted and watch how he treated people in everyday moments.

I took that lesson to heart, visualizing the life, partnership, and family I desired. Her words gave me clarity and discernment, helping me walk away from relationships that didn't align with my values, and stayed in my head when I was tempted to settle. Mama made sure I didn't confuse material success with a good heart.

Twenty-six years, two businesses, my dream house, three boys (now men), and a dog named Buddy later, I know for sure: her wisdom didn't just guide my heart—it blessed my life beyond measure.

"Keep living."

I used to hate when Mama said that—mainly because it followed my bold declarations of, "I would never…" Like most Gen X daughters raised by Silent Generation mothers, she couldn't fully imagine the freedoms we'd gain, though she prayed for them. I remember sitting in the bank, watching her—credit spotless, yet still needing my father's signature to buy a house.

I went beyond her wildest dreams: the first in my family to graduate from college, earn a Ph.D., become a professor, and start my own business.

With every milestone, I thought times were changing for good. But mama just gave me that knowing look and said, "Keep living."

The older I get, the more I understand. She wasn't being dismissive—she was passing down hard-earned wisdom. As a Black woman, she was reminding me: progress comes, but so does backlash. Rights won can be lost. Doors kicked open can be quietly closed again.

Watching rights she fought for rolled back—and rights I took for granted threatened—I finally get it. Her words have anchored, steeled, and humbled me.

Keep living wasn't a warning. It is a rallying cry—and a blueprint for my becoming.

My mother was shaped by an America that didn't always honor her agency or value Black women's wisdom. Her sayings became both shield and sword—giving me humor, discernment, and the courage to keep living. As a Black woman who endured hardship, her deepest wish was for me to live in possibility.

Generationally, we've sometimes felt worlds apart. But with time, I've learned to hold space for both our truths—knowing she survived so I could thrive. Thriving with eyes wide open and a heart sharpened by discernment while moving through this world with the armor of her lived wisdom.

I understand now: life will always come with challenges. Yet, like her, I'll keep showing up, keep pressing forward, and keep living.

Because in the end, that's her greatest lesson: **"Survive so you can thrive."**

Affirmation:

I AM RESILIENT!

Angela Jean-Louis, Ph.D.

Dr. Angela Jean-Louis is a storyteller, social impact leader, and advocate for midlife audacity.

As the first in her family to earn a Ph.D., she honors her roots while building generational legacy through education, entrepreneurship, and empowerment.

Dr. Angela is the founder of the Leadership Concepts Institute and author of the upcoming book *Thrive on Purpose:Lessons from the Ancestors.*

A wife of 26 years, serial entrepreneur, and mother of three sons, she draws strength from her Southern upbringing and the timeless wisdom passed down from her mother, Annette Cain. Inspired by her framework of the same name, Dr. Angela's mission is simple but powerful:to help women do better, be better, and have better® —starting from within.

You can download her free eBook, *How to Use the Power of Visualization to Thrive on Purpose,* and join her Thrive on Purpose™ membership at @drangelacoaches.com.

Humming Her Own Tune… Martha's Story

By

Dr. AudreyAnn C. Moses

Humming Her Own Tune...
Martha's Story

Martha

"Joyce" Tolbert Coats

> “Life is easier than you think, all you have to do is accept the impossible. Do without the indispensable and bear the intolerable and be able to smile at anything.”(Author Unknown)
>
> “Ye shall know the truth and the truth shall make you free.”
>
> John 8:32

Loving our mother was a choice we made on our own, not because she made it easy.

She was born Martha Tolbert on October 20th, 1933, during the Great Depression. She was a twin, but her sister Mary only survived a few months. In her thirties, she gave herself a middle name— “Joyce.” When she passed, we had to put Joyce in the obituary so people knew it was her. Until the age of 10, she was an only child. Her sisters, Ann and Helen, were born years later. Though they loved each other, our aunts were “sisters” together—apart from our mom.

Times were hard, but she had a decent life. She grew up in Greenwood, South Carolina, when bathrooms were outside, water had to be toted in, and cooking was done on wood-burning stoves. A coal stove heated the house. It was a good life.

She married her high school sweetheart, Howard Coats, Sr., and they moved from South Carolina to Philadelphia, Pennsylvania, where we lived until 1969. They are both sleeping in Jesus now.

Humming Her Own Tune... Martha's Story

Our mother chose to be a stay-at-home mom. She taught my sisters and me how to sew and cook. She was incredibly creative. She could sew anything—making all our clothes, for both the boys and the girls. I remember she grew tired of our old couch. One day we came home to find she'd cut it in half and was reupholstering it. She turned the two halves into corner chairs. They were beautiful and lasted 20 more years.

Once, she wanted something new to wear to an event. Without a pattern, she used paper bags and newspaper to make a pattern. In about three days, she made a matching dress, coat, and hat. She was the Queen of the Ball. She was known to tear apart an old dress and remake it into something entirely new. If born in today's world, she would've been a designer—especially for women. We each have keepsakes she created: blankets; embroidered, knitted, or crocheted items; and tablecloths.

She and my dad were both excellent cooks, and she was an awesome baker. She made bread about once a week. Homemade bread, rolls, and biscuits were always in the house. She tried to teach me how to make yeast rolls, but that gene skipped me and landed on my son, now a professional chef and baker.

My dad always kept a vegetable garden, so we had fresh vegetables year-round. What we didn't eat, she froze or canned. She also loved flowers, indoors and outdoors. My brother Garrett and I inherited this love from her, along with preserving garden food the way she taught me.

Both of my parents loved reading and music. There were books in every room.

When I thought about what to write, the Holy Spirit reminded me to include the memories of my siblings—Lyndia Belcher, Howard Coats, Jr. "June," Garrett Coats, and Marcus Tolbert. Our sister Iris passed away December 24, 2021.

Lyndia's memories, "Although she had few friends, the ones who stuck by her loved her unconditionally. Her mix of friends was a strange lot —old and young, men and women, all races, creeds, and nationalities. Later in life, Mom began to forget things, and we realized she had Alzheimer's.

There were good times. I remember us dancing in the floor to the radio, laughing while Mom sang along. She had a beautiful voice, like Mahalia Jackson. We sang at churches while she played the piano (self-taught).

We never had big birthday parties. She'd bake a cake and have fun snacks but only invited our cousins. She said we were enough for a party.

She was talented. After taking a short night course on drawing, she began sketching portraits and landscapes. I'd see her gazing at something or someone, and later she'd draw it. I once asked how she remembered it. She said she drew it in her mind first, so she could see it clearly. Her work looked just like the original. A shop in town wanted to hang her work, but she wouldn't allow it. She didn't think it would be appreciated. She drew for her own satisfaction." (Our brother Howard inherited her drawing gene.)

Our mother loved writing—poetry and thoughts. She never published, and sadly, I've only found one or two of her writings and drawings. If we find more, I will publish them for her. I can honestly say I inherited her creative, artistic gene.

My brothers are men of few words, but I recall them saying our mom lived the best life she could under the circumstances. Maybe one day, they'll let me write a story for them about her.

Martha was deeply loved by us, her sisters, grandchildren, nieces, nephews, friends, and most importantly, by Jesus. I know I will see her on that great day when Jesus raises us from our sleep to live with Him in Heaven forever.

Affirmation:

I KNOW I AM THE DAUGHTER OF THE MOST HIGH GOD.

Dr. AudreyAnn C. Moses

Certified Christian Life Coach
Mental Wellness Counselor
Bestselling Author | US Navy (Retired)

Dr. AudreyAnn C. Moses is dedicated to empowering individuals to achieve personal and professional growth. With a deep passion for community development, she actively participates in programs that foster meaningful transformation.

As an experienced workshop and program facilitator, she brings insight and encouragement to those seeking positive change. Her work extends beyond coaching. She is a five-time bestselling author and recipient of multiple literary awards.

Her portfolio includes eight published novels, and professional magazine articles focused on personal growth, self-care, and transformation.

Dr. Moses and her husband, Leonard (Navy Vietnam Veteran) live in Greenwood, South Carolina. They have four adult children, ten grandchildren, and two great-grandsons—life experiences that inspire her stories about Christian family dynamics, love, and devotion to one another and to God. To connect with Dr. Moses please visit https://transitionlifecoach4u.com.

Chapter 8

A Letter to Momma

By

Clintoria Session

A Letter to Momma

Brenda Lou Wakefield

> "No matter what we encounter, never forget that we serve a mighty God."

Dear Momma,

Life has been so very different since you transitioned, and words could never properly explain how I miss you and long to have just one more conversation with you. Time seemed to stand still for a while, and now I can't believe that it's been 26 years without my biggest supporter and role model. I've often thought about what we would be doing if you were still here, and I can't help but to feel some type of way when I see daughters with their moms simply enjoying life. I somehow feel robbed of the years that we didn't have. I was a 26-year-old young wife and mom when you transitioned. I wasn't ready to do life without you.

Thank you for being so selfless; you gave so much of yourself to those around you. Even during your last month of life, you made sure that you were in the hospital room with me as I delivered my second child. Momma, you just don't know how much this meant to me. You had a way of bringing a sense of calm and peace. You always made me feel like I could accomplish anything. You were able to see your first two grandsons, but I've had a third son named Titus O'Ryan who is 19 now and a sophomore in college. I make sure that I speak of you so that he knows who you are even if he didn't have the chance to meet you.

A Letter to Momma

You would be so proud of the boys. All three of them have a love for God and humanity. Micah frequently mentions how much he misses you and wishes you were still here. Dushuan is doing well and living in Mississippi with his kids. He misses you terribly.

The day you went to be with Jesus was one of the darkest days of my life. The pain and emptiness were indescribable. I was in such a dark place for 6 months after your passing. I know this isn't what you would want for me. I can still hear you telling me after you received your cancer diagnosis, "Sister, no matter what, always remember we serve a mighty God." Momma, I have to be honest, I was really angry with God after you passed but I know it was your prayers that carried me through that dark time because I couldn't pray for myself nor did I have the desire. You were my favorite girl who I admired so much. Your strength during times of adversity, how you continued to show love to those who talked about you and mistreated you and how you never lost faith in God even as you battled cancer are to be admired. Your heart was so big, and you were the glue for so many and missed by all who knew you.

Momma, I know life was challenging as a single parent, and we didn't make it easy at times. Many times I'm sure we were clueless of your struggles because you were intentional with not placing burdens on us as kids. We didn't have much money, but we were rich in love. You made sure that we had what we needed and some of what we wanted. You sacrificed so much to ensure that we had better opportunities than what you were afforded as a kid. One of my fondest memories is seeing you kneeling beside your bed each night praying to God and every morning you sitting on the bed talking to Him as we started our day. There have been many times in my life when I stop and say, "Momma, you were right." You always said that life is a good teacher. God has been so good to me, and I just wish you were here to share the journey with me. I have a successful career in Human Resources and travel to countries that I never dreamt of. With each success, I think of you and hope that I am making you proud. My heart of giving back to those in need came from you, and I am so grateful.

Momma, thank you for every tear you cried for us, every prayer you whispered and for never missing a football game, competition, or whatever it was we were involved in as kids. Thank you for every lesson. Momma, you will always be the piece of my heart that resides in heaven and yes, we do serve a mighty God. Love you beyond words and keep watching over us.

Affirmation:

I AM ENOUGH.

Clintoria Session

Author, HR Professional,

Coach, Minister

Clintoria Wakefield Session was born and raised in Seneca, South Carolina. She is an energetic, caring and dedicated Human Resources professional with over 25 years of experience who is certified to facilitate, speak, train and coach in the areas of leadership development, personal development, and career development.

She is also the CEO of Coach Tori Empowers, equipping others to excel both on a personal and professional level. Her passion is to assist others with breaking through barriers in order to live their best life.

She and her husband, Samuel Session, Jr., have been married for 32 years and have three extraordinary sons and one wonderful daughter in love.

Chapter 9

Seeds of Faith: The Garden My Mother Grew

By
Debbie Woodbury, MPA, SHRM-CP, CPRP

Seeds of Faith: The Garden My Mother Grew

Enid Rose Maitland

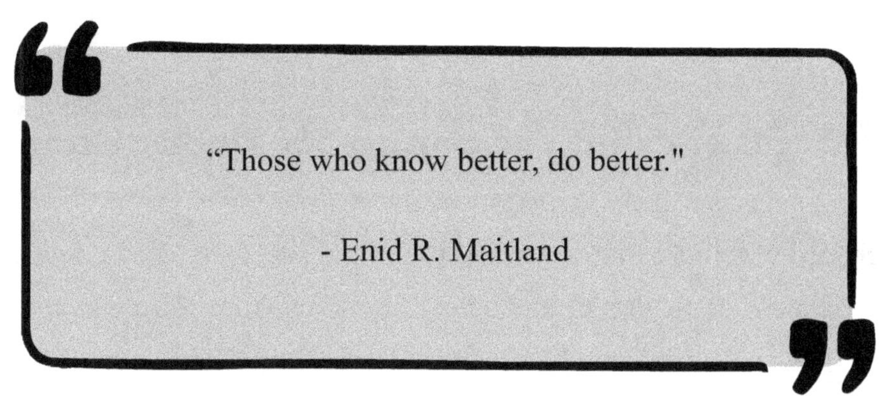

A master gardener, my mother, Enid Rose Maitland, lived to plant. She planted love. She planted faith. She planted flowers. And everything she planted grew and flourished.

Born in Saint Andrew, Jamaica, she was diagnosed with a congenital heart condition. Doctors doubted she would survive past age two. But God had other plans for her life.

Thirty years later, Mommy learned about a job opportunity in the United States and pursued it with faith and confidence. She left Jamaica with her clothes and a few dollars to her name. When she arrived, no one came to pick her up from the airport. But God sent two Good Samaritans to help her. She decided to stay in the country and find another job. She began a new life.

She was a nurturer. Mommy never quit gardening, heart condition and all. She knew that she was supposed to take it easy, and for her, that meant not getting caught. Her neighbor shared that as soon as her health aide departed for the day, Mommy would sneak out of the house and into the yard. That's my mommy - quietly rebellious, wildly faithful, always giving.

Seeds of Faith: The Garden My Mother Grew

Her yard was more than a garden; it was her sanctuary. You could smell the richness of fresh soil and sweet blossoms from the sidewalk. Red roses and pink hibiscus bloomed under her care. The tall sunflowers danced in the breeze. Her garden was cultivated with intention and care, as if her strength was rooted in planting.

Mommy turned every hardship into fertile ground, planting each challenge with prayer. She sowed kindness through countless acts. She watered our dreams with late-night prayers. She pruned our bad habits with discipline and high standards. She cultivated a deep faith that never ran dry. She never made plans without first saying, “If God spares my life.” She didn't just believe in God; she walked with Him, and she taught me to do the same.

Every Sunday, we were in church. Not just sitting but serving. Choir, Sunday school, acolyte duties, you name it, I did it. Sundays were sacred; there was no cooking, no cleaning, and no work on the Sabbath. She is the inspiration behind my walk with Christ. She taught me that faith without works is dead. She lived her belief in God every day by caring for the sick, feeding the hungry, and giving to those in need, even when she had very little herself. Mommy showed me that faith is not just about belief but about action. It's about living your values and making a positive impact on the world around you. Her heart was full of Christ-centered love. I miss her prayers when I travel. She would always say, "Be safe, watch people, and God go with you." Her prayers wrap me in God's protection.

She instilled in me the importance of self-respect and hard work. Nothing worth having comes easy; that's something she made sure I knew. She taught me that the real garden is in the people you raise and the lessons you leave behind. Although she is no longer here, she left a plethora of lessons behind.

What I miss most is the delicacy of her passion. She was like her name, Rose. Beautiful, fragrant, but with thorns that reminded you that she didn't play. Discipline? She believed in it. If "reach out and touch someone" were a person, it was her. And don't get me started on the infamous yardstick I found while cleaning her house. It measured fabric and attitudes. But beneath that firmness was a selfless heart filled with grace. She simply did what was right because it was right.

Mommy defied every odd. Her cardiologist often looked at her in awe, as she lived independently well into her 80s, taking care of herself and still tending to her beloved garden. He called her an anomaly.

To me, she was simply Mommy, the embodiment of strength, resilience, and love. Her heart, though medically limited, overflowed with boundless love. She taught me that love isn't just a feeling; it's a verb. It's about how you show up for others when no one is watching; that's where true character is revealed. She instilled in me the value of hard work, self-reliance, and the importance of earning what you have. She taught me how to save. "You don't have to spend every penny you make. And everything you see, you don't need to have."

Mommy, I am forever grateful to you.

- For every seed you planted.
- Every weed you pulled.
- Every storm you braved.
- Every prayer you whispered.

Your garden is still growing. And because of you, I will keep planting, keep tending, and keep believing. Your love lives on. Your legacy grows stronger. And I'll never stop telling the world what my momma taught me.

Affirmation:

I AM A LEADER, NOT A FOLLOWER.

Debbie Woodbury, MPA, SHRM-CP, CPRP

Founder and Managing Director of Meritology Institute

Debbie Woodbury is a leadership development and career coach, author, and professional speaker who empowers others to grow, lead, and thrive. With over 20 years of leadership experience in public service, Debbie is a lifelong learner who holds numerous professional certifications and has a passion for helping others succeed. She is also the founder and Managing Director of Meritology Institute, where she creates transformative learning experiences that drive growth for both individuals and organizations.

A native of Washington, DC, Debbie draws inspiration from her roots and the invaluable wisdom of her Jamaican mother, whose guidance instilled in her a deep sense of resilience, faith, and perseverance. Guided by purpose and compassion, her work is rooted in the principles of equity and empowerment. She remains devoted to honoring her mother's legacy of faith, generosity, and resilience. Outside of facilitating workshops and coaching professionals, Debbie finds joy in writing, traveling, and embracing her role as a proud mother to three young men.

Letter to the Reader

Dear Reader,

I hope that the love and wisdom shared on these pages inspires you to be a better mother, daughter, sister, niece, aunt, and friend. All of us need a mother, whether by blood or by love. I hope that you let the mothers in your life know what they mean to you and share their love and wisdom with the daughters in your life.

May we all know love, show love, and be loved in a way that makes us better to everyone we meet . May we never hesitate to give love where it's needed. It matters. Love is never wasted when it's shared. And mothers are proof of that.

Be blessed. Keep Winning!
Regina Sunshine

Personal Scripture Affirmations

I was created in the image of God.

Greater is He that is within me than he that is in the world.

I will praise thee; for I am fearfully and wonderfully made.

I am more than a conqueror through Him that loves me.

I can do all things through Christ who strengthens me.

If God is for me, who can be against me.

God has not given me a spirit of fear, but of power, and love and a sound mind.

I am the temple of the Holy Spirit, and the Spirit of God dwells in me.

I am worthy of the call God has on my life.

I am worthy of living the life I was created for.

I am worthy of the dreams God has placed in my heart.

I Am Worthy

Personal General Affirmations

I was born to win.

I am more than a conqueror.

I was created for greatness.

I was born to be victorious.

I will achieve my dreams.

I can be anything I choose.

I can do anything I set my mind to.

I am a champion.

I am worthy of the best things in life.

I am worthy of the dreams in my heart.

I am worthy of living a great life.

I am worthy.

Partner Affirmations

God loves you just the way you are.

You are beautiful because you were created in love.

You were fearfully and wonderfully made.

You have the seeds of greatness within you.

You were born to live a victorious life.

You are brilliant, gorgeous, talented, and fabulous.

You Are Worthy.

About the Organizer

Regina Sunshine Robinson is an Empowerment Specialist who focuses on writing, publishing, motivational speaking, coaching, and consulting. She is the CEO of Regina Sunshine Global Network. Regina Sunshine

is a graduate of North Carolina A&T State University with a Bachelor of Science in Chemical Engineering. She is an award-winning author, talk show host, and community activist. Regina is the author of two books, *Regina Sunshine State of Mind* and *Chasing Sunshine.* Regina is a 3- Time Chicken Soup for the Soul Contributor, having stories published in editions *Curvy & Confident, Be You, and Self-Care Isn't Selfish.* She is a lover of people and servant to God's people. Her personal motto is "It's Not Over Til I Win," and she wins when she sees others winning. Contact her at ReginaSunshine.com.

www.ingramcontent.com/pod-product-compliance
Lightning Source LLC
LaVergne TN
LVHW010616110826
845149LV00003B/934